I Decided
to Be Free

I Decided to Be Free

NEW EDITION 2021

Connie C. Torres

Library of Congress Control Number:		2016915824
ISBN:	Hardcover	978-1-5065-3711-5
	Softcover	978-1-5065-3709-2
	eBook	978-1-5065-3710-8

Print information available on the last page.

Rev. date: 25/05/2021

To order additional copies of this book, please contact:
Palibrio
1663 Liberty Drive
Suite 200
Bloomington, IN 47403
Toll Free from the U.S.A 877.407.5847
Toll Free from Mexico 01.800.288.2243
Toll Free from Spain 900.866.949
From other International locations +1.812.671.9757
Fax: 01.812.355.1576
orders@palibrio.com
829616

CONTENTS

II
"THE SPIRITUAL WORLD"

DECIDE TO BE FREE = HAPPINESS

"Build your world of happiness with moments of joy,
transforming the negative into the positive,
while life teaches you to feel happy despite the circumstances."
Connie C. Torres :)

INTRODUCTION

"I decided to be free to elevate my physical life experiences on a spiritual level." I have been encouraged to grow up by a series of thoughts born in my soul, and and I have guided my life in many enlightened beings' directions. I embrace and rely on my spiritual sense of life to help me understand this complicated world, and make my imperfect world seem less scary. We all have the power to change our world and community for the better, if we trust in our instincts to change the things we can and accept the ones we cannot change. The ability to listen to our soul will enable us to become at peace with everyday life, but daily life tasks and obsessions within the material world. "I decided to be free" has brought me a personal renaissance by feeling so glad. I let you know the impact this decision has made on me and celebrate life by sharing my essence towards humanity. *"My happiness is to motivate people to fight their innermost fears and prejudices. To avoid negative consequences to our lives; we need to firmly maintain our convictions through our hearts, and not be manipulated by our minds."* "I invite you to explore this literary garden, as a gift of life, so that everyone may be happy in a world filled with love and peace."

I

LIFE AND LOVE

HAPPINESS

"Happiness is the perfect harmony desired by human beings," but what makes some people happy does not necessarily translate to other people's happiness. Each person has their values that coincide with this notion of being happy. *"Complaining is a negative energy when you don't feel happy."* Negative energy will lead you to a world of slavery; doubt and fear will make you feel even more unhappy. You should not allow these forces to dominate your mind and just think: *"Things happen the way they should be,"* and accept life's consequences with serenity. Neither the joys nor the sorrows last forever, so we have to make ourselves happy in good or in bad times since life is about maintaining an emotional balance in any situation. Being happy is not as difficult as most people think. The real difficulty is trying to understand how to acquire the wisdom to reach this level of happiness, in which your *"attitude towards life is the true path of happiness."* Your heart achieves a solid foundation of love that will allow you to live the way you want.

"Give love, be tender, collect affections, cultivate your inner peace and build a solid foundation for your soul, then just wait for happiness."

You should reflect on your actions if you desire to live in harmony with your mind and spirit, to discover the potential in your soul. Once you begin to control your thoughts about your problems, you will not feel frustrated by unexpected situations. You will realize that any difficult moment is fleeting and temporary, and you will only have the wisdom to change the things you can. You will be able to confront each difficult situation by focusing on realistic solutions through meditation.

"If you believe it, you reach it, but only if you have realistic goals, then, these goals will lead you to satisfaction."

"Eternal Happiness does not exist; only the attitude towards the sense of life makes the difference."

WHAT MAKES ME HAPPY?

You are the only one who has the responsibility to make you happy. You need to meditate in your inner self to determine if your lifestyle is related to your notion of happiness. In this way, you can add the activities or situations that bring you joy and subtract those that take away from your happiness. You will be able to see if you are accomplishing your goals, still keeping in mind that: ***"You will never feel pleased all the time. You cannot achieve a perfect level of happiness in this imperfect world."*** Nonetheless, it is always good to push yourself towards reaching new goals, and taking on new challenges in your life. Begin working towards your goals of happiness; you will feel happy each time you complete an objective.

I firmly respect and believe:

1. *Love;*
2. *Smile;*
3. *Music;*
4. *Family and friends;*
5. *Honesty;*
6. *Generosity;*
7. *Forgive others;*
8. *Living things, animals, and plants;*
9. *Take care of the environment;*

10. ***Respect others' feelings; and***
11. ***Be spiritual, Positive attitude.***

You have to find your own happiness goals in your inner self, but let's consider your real feelings and attitudes towards life to revitalize your heart.

"You search for happiness in people, places, and other material things in this imperfect world. Happiness lies within yourselves, so you have to take a look inside to find your inner peace."

EMOTIONS

"Emotion is an instinctive state of mind deriving from one's circumstances, mood or relationships with others." Take control of your emotions, especially when thoughts and actions are in synchronization disorder. This disorder happens when you experience an emotional imbalance, and nothing seems to work out the way you want. You will lose control of everything worked not only material loss but also a spiritual setback on the road to your happiness. This emotional issue might lead you to lose perception of your life. Before reaching an emotional crisis, your heart will activate warning alarms to provide you with relief for not letting yourself sink into this emotional pit. Your gut tells you when something is going wrong, don't choose to ignore it, or you will fall into a state of desperation. You lose control of your emotions which hinders your progress towards happiness. *"Your feelings can't be under the control of others or being allowed to influence your thoughts."* Follow your heart to maintain an emotional balance to accept all challenges in life You should love yourself first and then continue to love others despite everything negative brought against you. Remember, nobody else feels your heart and inner soul. Therefore, if you are heartbroken, suffering, and sad, it is not worth losing control of your emotional balance for anyone or anything. Do not add more sadness to your life. Just cling to those good feelings which are closest to your heart. Don't surrender your heart to those people who seek to injure your

feelings. Learning how to deal with your emotions successfully is how you discover the path of happiness.

"Follow your heart to maintain an emotional balance. It will allow you to accept all challenges in life."

BALANCE YOUR EMOTIONS

Sensitive people feel plenty of emotions hard to manage in challenging life aspects, such as politics, economic and social problems worldwide. Many situations in life will interfere with your emotional balance. You should not yield to the pressures of sentimentality to control your feelings; you should start living a balanced life with no great expectations. Therefore, you must know who you are and where you will obtain the best results in your emotional life. ***"Being confident makes you feel authentic."*** In this material world, you have to accommodate your lifestyle according to your values as a human being. And always keep the freedom of mind closest to reality, not feeling scared to face life situations that make you grow emotionally.

"If you dream of a better world, start creating yours by helping others. Sure, you will never be able to save the entire world at once, but you will be able to improve life in your community."

SHOULD WE CRY?

Crying is a natural human phenomenon in moments of intense emotions. *"We know that tears clean and soothe our sadness."* Tears fall just as rain falls from storm clouds in the sky. Rain cleanses the world naturally, then the sun reappears, and the atmosphere becomes blue again. *"Nature is renewed and cleaned after a rainfall, as it happens in our soul after a period of crying, we become calm and feel better after a good cry."* When you feel sad or confused, allow yourself to let it out with an outpour of tears. Crying will also help you to relieve frustration and anger-the negative emotions which can injure your heart. Suffering combined with bitterness changes into hatred, and hatred is cancer that leads your soul to a life filled with unhappiness. Hearts are full of love, but if your heart is full of hatred, it will lead to all sorts of problems in your life. Many people suffer from this disease called hatred without even realizing it; they become prisoners of a frustrated and miserable life.

FEELING DISAPPOINTED

We often become disappointed when we place unrealistic ideals upon people or situations as pretending that people are perfect. Still, they are only humans and bound to make mistakes. Instead, we should accept people for who they are, mortal beings who have virtues and defects. The mind fabricates unreal notions, but the heart creates real love. The reason transports you to a fictional world and flies like a bird for a short period. Still eventually, you realize that your expectations are just a bitter dream. You better trust in your feelings to transport you to a place where dreams can become a reality. Your heart always gives you divine messages which bring long-lasting happiness. Your mind often tends to create doubt when you make decisions influenced by impulses. Impulses are momentary emotions that confuse us. Besides, feelings always remain solid and never die; they merely transform. Therefore, suffering is an accumulation of resentment, hatred, envy, and frustration injuring your soul. Such negative feelings lead you to lower your self-esteem by destroying your spiritual purity.

"To avoid feeling sad, don't let your imagination run wild. Conclude to explain those things which you can't understand, just accept them as they are."

"You learn from your mistakes, no matter how many times you've failed. You should gain wisdom from your shortcomings and add valuable experience to your life by learning from failure."

People who succumb to hatred:

a) *Have not discovered their inner world;*
b) *Don't make any effort in trying to discover their true personality;*
c) *Live only in the outer world;*
d) *Don't care about other people; and*
e) *Become submerged in a dark world, in which the light of hope no longer shines and in which love has no room to breathe.*

"When you maintain your authenticity and remain true to yourself, you will preserve your dignity long after your physical life is over."

To avoid negative feelings, love yourself as much as possible.

You must meditate:

1. *Think positively and peacefully;*
2. *Let problems be solve by themselves;*
3. *Past is already gone, just live today;*
4. *Forgive and forget;*
5. *Be happy;*
6. *Be realistic;*
7. *Be a human being; and*
8. *Respect others.*

When you can balance your emotions, any situations of sadness, sorrow, or frustration will eventually lead you to spiritual growth and a greater understanding of your inner self. This growth will add valuable experience to self-discovery on this journey which we call life.

"Don't let sorrow live in your heart, learn from it, but don't let it be part of your lifestyle; strengthen your heart to let the sorrow leave forever."

RELATIONSHIPS

In any relationship, separations are hard to manage, and break-ups occur even if one of the two is still in love. Many factors can break up a relationship, caused by the lack of love, respect, comprehension, and care. A broken relationship starts inside the couple; nobody else causes a separation, it is involved by two. Separation is usually better than maintaining a relationship filled with a hellish world of indifference, disrespect, and distrust. A functional relationship full of love doesn't break apart easily; instead, many factors cause the foundation to collapse. In such cases, neither partner alone is to blame for the separation- the base was probably never solid. Neither partner started a relationship with the idea that they would be flowing down a river of loneliness and destruction. Thus, you need to face and acknowledge the reality of separation.

"To prove your love to someone, let the freedom flow to grow as a human being, to feel, think and let your partner choose their way. If they both feel happy, love has proved."

When children are involved as a result of a parent's broken relationship, both of you should be ready to manage the situation and focus on attending to your children's needs. Give them an honest explanation and let them know as parents, you will always be; they will understand it. Seek psychological help if they need it for your kids to maintain their emotional balance. Psychological support and guidance kids and adolescents the best chance of dealing with such situations. A forced relationship provides a style of life that is not healthy nor happy. Some people cling to a relationship where love no longer exists, even if their partner no longer cares or loves somebody else. This attitude makes their self-esteem plummet, and they go through the hell of an emotional imbalance. As human beings, you should take this experience as a lesson learned to grow emotionally. When a partner looks for someone else, love has changed, and feelings flow differently direction. It is over! Your partner no longer feels the light of love because there isn't anymore an emotional connection. A functional relationship with feelings of love, respect, loyalty, and trust, will last longer by supporting each other unconditionally to walk together in the path of love.

A functional relationship:

1. *We should smile and feel full of joy which comes from our heart and doesn't allow anyone to erase the smile from our lips;*
2. *We should maintain a relationship with our partner based on love, communication and mutual respect;*
3. *We should create an emotional balance in which both of us can enjoy and share moments of joy and excitement;*
4. *We should have the freedom to be able to choose what makes us happy but also feel free to reject those things which don't provide us with happiness; and*
5. *We should be able to express our feelings in freedom.*

"When you maintain your authenticity and remain true to yourself, you will preserve your dignity long after your physical life is over."

"Don't try to change impossible situations if you remain calm, peace will come and problems resolve by themselves."

LOVE WILL ALWAYS BE LOVE

"Love is divinity, real, perfect, and the purest feeling in humanity which lives in your inner self and flows naturally." Love is a great virtue that becomes revealed through happiness; your heart feels and senses real love because you cannot possess love; it's a magical feeling that loses its charm when you try to manage it. In love, there are no expectations because it is a feeling that flows naturally without an explanation to be given. If a love affair doesn't fit you, then you shouldn't waste time suffering over it; just simply accept consequences without feeling disappointment or betrayal. Understanding love is a feeling born in freedom, to live it as it is, and let it flow naturally like water. You never know where real love may be, just let it flow the day that comes.

"Love grows and reproduces when you let it flow itself in giving and getting back without fears or expectations."

THE WOUND OF LOVE

Love is a magical feeling, it flows when you never expect it, and it grows more potent in its pure and infinite nature. *"Time can heal the wound which love has caused after a relationship is over."* Sometimes circumstances in life will make you believe that love no longer exists, but that's not true. Your heart is full of love to give, but you never know when the love of your life will appear, you will recognize it when you fall in love. Life experience means to be in love unless once, trust in love, even if sometimes it does not work, just take it over, and start all over again, cause it is better to have suffered because of love than never to have loved at all. You need to experience the feeling of love without worrying about the consequences. You don't decide who to love or not; your heart is the one who dominates all of your emotions. The freedom to love and be loved makes you share in a relationship a bonding of love that can produce marvelous results.

"If you are devoted to your feelings, you will always be in love. Love flows like a river and expands it to the infinite like the stars in the sky."

WOMEN AND THEIR EMOTIONS

In the book "The Female Brain, author Lovann Brizadine explains that women have 11% more neurons than men. For this reason, women are better able to express their emotions. They are also able to remember emotional events in greater detail. Women can't think and act like men do when nature itself has created women and men differently. It is advantageous for women to have an advanced level of emotions. Still this difference complicates relationships with partners that don't emphasize on certain details the way certain women do. They create controversy because men and women are both living in the outside world in which the mind dominates. In the inner world, the heart needs to maintain individuality to respect everyone's spiritual concepts. In this inner world, men and women can reach a more harmonious and perfect relationship by feeling that each one can get along with the other.

"The functional couple will mirror each other in their reflection and will enjoy the full beauty of love."

RAISING YOUR SELF ESTEEM

"One of the saddest situations in life is to live without hope." If you have allowed life to pass you by without realizing it, it's because you don't love yourself. *"Don't let other people decide what makes you happy; wake up and enjoy your life being yourself."* Your happiness lives in your inner soul. Just believe in yourself to allow you to set everything in its proper place. Wisdom and confidence let you know what to do at the right moment and in specific situations. Focusing only on materialism will not provide you with long-lasting satisfaction. *"Your self-esteem will rise when your pure soul guides you to the inner self, and your self-confidence wakes up to celebrate the divine power of true love, which you have in your hands."* Therefore, this attitude attracts your life to focus the energy on your spiritual life balance with the external world. Today technology and Social Media have done wonders, creating practical options to meet goals in education and in the professional sphere, which is the key that opens the doors of opportunities of growing and progressing as human being to raise their self-esteem. As human beings, we all have to raise our self-esteem and self-confidence to be helpful in this society, in whatever roles we have to play in life.

"When you are proud of yourself, it means you are raising your self-esteem and taking care of your actions."

MATERIAL WORLD

"People in the material world "obsessively" only focus on possessing money, care for goods and luxury." "Living like this creates an imbalance in your inner peace." It doesn't mean that you cannot progress and achieve your goals towards your happiness, that it is perfectly normal, enforce yourself by working to have a better life according to your needs. I can say: *"You can step on whatever dream comes true if you want to make it real, but you should feel as happy as always, even if you don't materialize it." "To possess or not to possess doesn't matter because your values are on another level, and your essence as a human being makes you feel great."* You are a materialist if you live for possessing material things, can't live without those goods, or are willing to lose your dignity to achieve these possessions. It is prevalent to see convenience for progress being a factor for people in many situations. People don't know that losing pride simply means you have lost your identity so that nobody can trust you anymore.

Two worlds in one life:

Materialistic people focus on the external world and always feel disappointed not to achieve their goals; they need material things to feel happiness.

Spiritual people focus on their inner self, in everyday life, peaceful and full of light and love; they don't need material goods to feel happy. They are full of happiness.

A HUMAN BEING

"A human being is a distinguished animal with a superior mental development, power of articulate speech, created to love and be loved." A human being grows spiritual, then engages in society. In the modern world, each one was born to serve others no matter what. Still in reality, humans live in a world far away from harmony and care for others because the world is filled with lots of incentives from the heart. Every human is unique, authentic, free of mind, capable of creating a wonderful world on their side. Honest with their values to develop their skills they love, and preparing for their passion as a career that will bring them closer to happiness. All human beings exhibit behaviors differently. Some can feel love and care about others, some would like but don't do anything, some want to, but something doesn't match their intentions. Things don't work out the way they want. It does not mean they are not good human beings because they don't need to be recognized for any actions. Not everyone has the possibilities and resources, but some can help on their own if they want. Sadly we all have to deal in a material world, ruled by earthly minds whose values don't have the meaning of human rights.

"Humanity has resources for developing a world full of love, truth, and reality, but if we don't work in a community, we will never be able to balance the internal and external worlds."

"Forgive all because when you forgive, you bring peace to your soul and empty all resentments."

BEING UNIQUE

As human beings, we are born unique, but human personalities change in searching for happiness. Being unique is being authentic, not pretending to be somebody else or trying to be like someone is. Differences make an exciting variety of people to share. Most people expect your ideals of life to be theirs, to relate to you, so they can't respect your essence as a human being. This behavior is typical in the world we live in now. When we meet people who have never discovered their inner self and didn't feel the freedom of being themselves, we understand that we came into this world to be happy as individuals. We don't have to suffer all these negative feelings from others. We create as unique beings but similar in terms of capacity to feel. We all are humans, and we all have heart feelings to love each other and develop our skills to be successful.

"You can think and feel differently without affecting anybody, just respect one another's feelings, their dreams, and their ideologies of life."

"The most important thing in life is love along with respect. This divine love joins humanity, couples, families, and friends."

"Being unique is not being selfish; it is simply someone you can trust."

Being a dignified person makes you a trustworthy human being. You don't have to prove who you are to anybody and your actions speak for themselves. Sometimes, people force you to live under their feelings, encouraging you to lower your self-esteem for you will never feel proud of yourself. Who loves you will will love you to the end, accept you as you are, and respect your values. Therefore, be proud of yourself, and your environment will be balanced and full of peace to find yourself listening to the music of your heart and soul.

"The most important recognition you can get in your whole life is the one you can give to yourself."

"Dignity is like becoming yourself and living a peaceful life according to your emotions and feelings."

ATTITUDE TOWARDS LIFE

Life is about making conscious choices throughout your lifetime, which will allow you to maintain a balance between your thoughts and your emotions, being careful not to cause an overflow of either or risk falling into an emotional situation. *"Living your life means following your dreams while you are learning lessons and growing emotionally." "The attitude towards life must be concerned in living as a human being, conscious that life is not forever."* Every piece of your life puzzle is what is happening worldwide, you have to try to connect the parts, but as soon as you are setting the pieces, you will find out that some of them don't fit together. Therefore, you must place the pieces aside and keep checking with the right ones. You must never refuse to learn and understand the divine messages that the universe flows in your favor. In all situations, your attitude towards it determines how easy or hard it can be. It is essential to maintain a positive attitude to deal with difficult situations in life. You should be strong enough never to give up, no matter how hard the problem may be to solve. Life is better if your attitude is positive, and you live as happily as you can, then you will be able to face life with joy. When you discover your inner world your life completely changes to better care of your inner self. Most people live in a rush and get distracted in this material world. They don't take care of their inner self. Carelessness is mainly the reason why humans have negative thoughts by creating things solely with their minds.

"You must change negatives into positives; sadness into happiness; hatred into love."

"In the material world, you will never find the truth, only in your inner world will you raise and reproduce love."

"Dreams sometimes are part of the hidden truths which exist in your subconscious."

LIFE AND LOVE

Life was created in the feeling of love, to love, and to live as human beings. Humanity felt love inside their hearts for the sense of life. Real love is authentic, and usually, the external world manipulates people's feelings into convenient issues. The feeling of love lives in your inner self, bringing you happiness as a valuable treasure to balance all difficulties in your daily life. The great leaders worldwide don't focus on improving love and peace for humanity to create a better world for a living; instead, they are involved only in economic and political issues. You can't change the world, but you can change your attitude towards your own life to create a better world.

"Change your attitude towards life to build a better world that helps your environment."

"If we treat each other with tenderness, we will be able to relax and trust each other. The world will truly become a more joyful and happy place."

IMPORTANT DECISIONS

"Important decisions affecting your life must be made when you are calm and serene by listening to your heartbeat." Your heart never lies and it will benefit you in the long run. If something goes wrong, it doesn't mean you made a bad decision; that means your right decision was not the right one for that situation. You will learn from it because you will always have a second chance. Life is a basis of learning, and if you make mistakes, it's because you are human, and life strengthens you. Time will tell in the future if you made the right decision or not. *"Always be calm,"* because if you worry, anxiety will take control of your emotions. It will be the worst moment to make an important decision; your mind will not be clear and sensate, your mind will be confused, and your emotional thoughts will be out of control. In this world you never know what is going to happen, just being alive is risky. For this reason, when you have to make an important decision that affects you for better or worse, make sure you feel focused and relaxed.

"As a human being, it is easy living, but human's behavior makes it complicated."

"We are blessed with a fantastic mind and a lovely heart to decide whether we want to live in a complicated material world or a peaceful inner world."

FEARS

"Fears are negative feelings that bring negative vibes to your life and also attract bad energy in your environment." You will take away your chances at success, and you will be too afraid to take any risks to succeed in life. Fear will not let you mature as a human being; you will be unable to learn anything because you will not be open to teaching or being taught. People who are afraid and suffer from fear will never be able to live a life. It is natural to feel fear when you have to make any decision that affects your own life, but it is part of living in this world. You just have to feel comfortable with who you are--it is a good sign that leads your life in the best direction for you. In the real world not every problem has a solution. If you can solve it, let it flow as naturally as possible, and accept the outcome without forcing things to happen the way you expect because reality is the truth. You cannot change it; just take responsibility for your feelings.

EMOTIONAL HEALTH

Emotional well-being refers to the dynamic quality and individual experiences. Maintaining good emotional health depends on dealing with difficult situations in a level headed manner as a human being. Be relaxed and calm to make good decisions and balance your emotional health. You must be concerned with emotional and physical care to create a healthy balance between your body and soul. It is necessary to be physically healthy to feel comfortable and maintain good emotional health keeping you fit to deal with difficult situations in your environment. When people feel emotionally OK, their body functions equally in good health. Getting ill can result from emotional feelings disorder that lets your soul feel unhealthy; it is a terrible consequence for your body system. You should always combine balanced meals and exercise to cater to your body's needs. The wisdom of being healthy will bring you happiness daily.

"Be healthy in mind and body, give yourself that feeling of life."

"A leader does not mean to follow. A leader will influence your behavior to become a better person and encourage you by examples of freedom."

"Only the truth will make you feel happy inside. Lies do not have absolute power; they only offer a weak ladder to success by putting you on the wrong path to real happiness."

II

"THE SPIRITUAL WORLD"

SPIRITUALITY

"Spirituality is the divinity, the truth, the light, and the peace which comes from the conscious awareness of our creator." It is an endless opportunity for us to renew ourselves and to know that we can all become as great as we want to be. Spirituality is love and peace in our inner self that provides us a stable base for knowing and loving ourselves. Our heart takes excellent care of the pet in silence, soothing it when hurt because our life depends on this feeling of love. The world is afflicted, damaged, and corrupted by human behaviors, responsible for this condition. We must become more aware of our world's neglected diseases to open our minds positively. Human beings need to control their thoughts to stop being blocked and dominated by negative things that are not pure or even real. Spirituality can open the doors to the divine and real through meditation.

"To live in harmony, we must accept that everything flows naturally; we must remain calm and peaceful."

SPIRITUAL WORLD

"We all were born spiritual," humans carry spirituality deep within their souls even if they do not practice it. Spirituality opens the door to the truth with honest and pure love. Spirituality exists inside all of us, but we just have to dig deep to uncover it. To be spiritual, we need to nurture ourselves from the inside to listen to our hearts. A spiritual person rigorously cares for their soul and keeps far away from the outside world. Fear cannot intimidate a spiritual person. The opinions of the outside world are too weak to distract this person's mind and heart. Spiritual people can remain calm in any adverse situation because they are convinced that everything in life goes through cycles.

"Cultivate your spirit and give it what it needs for your soul to remain calm and divine."

"You will live as happy as you want if your soul is pure and full of love."

"Be true to yourself cultivating your soul in the present; forget about the past and future."

MEDITATION

"Meditation is a constant emotional renovation in a balanced form that opens your eyes to light and truth." Mediation is disconnecting yourself from the outer world in order to discover a world of light where peace and harmony guide you in reaching an emotional balance. Meditation simplifies your inner life and energizes your outer life. Modern Science has resulted in many marvelous discoveries. But its scope is still limited compared to the vision of the spiritual world. There is a world full of mysteries not yet discovered, but science doesn't have access to this world. Science is powerless in reaching higher levels of the spiritual world. However, something spiritual can penetrate the daily world and recognize its mysteries within its inner vision. A spiritual person is an authentic idealist who doesn't build castles in the sky; instead, this person has their feet firmly planted on the ground. Meditation consists of an awakening through which you feel closer to the fountain of creation - what you can imagine and impossible to define. The enemy of peace is a distraction that makes us lose sight of achieving harmony in our life. Harmony is the power that we have within ourselves to achieve balance. The biggest distraction to harmony is the desire for possessions. The road to meditation helps you confront the fear of the unknown and the fantasy and illusion that overcomes us when we encounter peace and tranquility. A long path opens the door

to all possibilities of happiness to be the person who chooses the road to follow through meditation.

"Maintaining a calm state of mind means taking control of your thoughts without having an emotional overload."

BASIC MEDITATION

1. Choose a quiet and private place in your house;

2. Set up your room with incense, candles, and flowers; this will purify your interior environment and inspire you to meditate;

3. Sit quietly and maintain silence; and

4. Relax, concentrate and breathe; your respirations must be suitable for meditation: When you inhale, it feels like you are living cosmic energy, and when you exhale, it feels like you are discharging impurity from your inner self, all impure thoughts, ideas, and actions.

LAW OF ATTRACTION

"The law of attraction is a mental capacity using the power of your thoughts to materialize whatever into reality." If you believe it, you create it; you just need to focus on your ideals. Convictions deep inside your soul can visualize this happiness to become real. Your energy is in charge of attracting those good things you want and deserve in life. For this reason, you must concentrate on all items which are positive in your spirit. Fear creates an emotional breakdown and a loss of spiritual faith, which causes you to tumble into negative thoughts and emotions. Besides, if you are only attracted to material without a spiritual basis, you will never be guaranteed true or long-lasting satisfaction. If you seek, feel, and perceive who you are, you can experience the inner world to flourish in an immense universe of light without thinking about material possessions.

"The truth of light is the divine secret to happiness, and it is open to those people who are willing to change, believe and create."

EMOTIONAL BALANCE

You should be very grateful as a human being for the chance of living, for the air to breathe, the sunlight, the water to drink, family and friends. Sometimes you waste your energy on the pursuit of material things, not on matters that will contribute to your spiritual growth. *"Everything in life follows its own pace and doesn't stop flowing just because you have problems to solve."* You just have to face it and keep going; your heart is the motor of your spiritual life ready for you. If you accept the inevitable, you will understand the depth of life and let life flow. What has passed is the past, so you should focus your energy on spiritual recovery because life is about constant renovation for healthy growth and improving your attitude toward life. On the road of life, painful things happen to everyone's lifetime. Be positive and strong in the face of adversity to embrace the good things in life. Happiness consists of all your shared moments lived and written in the book of your life. You should enjoy and appreciate those good times you have lived through experiences that count as learned lessons. Experiences allow you to grow in wisdom and to become a better version of yourself.

"Emotional balance is the true happiness lighted by the inner force which will lead us in calm on the road of life."

YOUR INNER SELF

"Your inner self is who you are inside, your values, your purpose in life, motivations, and beliefs." This inner world defines your feelings and the capacity you have to accept, understand, forgive, and forget. The first step to find your inner self is to meditate; then, you can explore yourself. Decide to renounce the outer world, and reevaluate yourself as a human being focussing on the inner world where your heart; and soul reside. On the other hand, the material world contains an emptiness that can never replace spiritual satisfaction and gives false promises of happiness. The most significant wealth in life is love in your heart; you will not lack anything. Joy brings and attains inner peace, not only in romantic relationships but feelings in general. Love soothes life's difficulties and helps to learn the meaning of life, which softens the pain in all moments. All human beings are born in a spiritual state to reach an emotional balance.

"Trust in your feelings and your inner voice because in many cases you are receiving divine messages that your conscious mind could never understand."

"Happiness is in your inner soul and comes through encountering spiritual truth."

THE ROAD TO HAPPINESS

"There is no magical path to your happiness; you are the one who has to pave it, step by step, based on your values, to achieve your goals and expectations." As a human, you must grow up and feel comfortable being alone. You can live as happily as you want. You love yourself as long as life teaches you to survive and deal with all situations. You are emotionally balanced to place everything on the perfect site. The path to happiness is for all to walk alone, sometimes accompanied only as an option. In relationships, for example, couples face some everyday situations that bring one partner happiness and don't bring joy to the other, but this causes an imbalance in coexistence. Teams shouldn't delegate their wellness to others, like: "You do what makes him happy" and "He does what makes you happy," instead of choosing to be happy as both of them are. Couples' relationships need to feel the freedom to consolidate real happiness. Each one should look for happiness inside himself/herself, but a couple of respect and accept each other's strengths and faults. Respecting the individuality of your partner is what makes functional couples last long. This understanding will lead your heart to infinite love on the way to happiness.

"We live to feel happiness individually; accompanied is only an option."

"Happiness is based on freedom as an individual."

"We were born with innate feelings of love, which determine our values."

"Hatred is a major obstacle in your attempt to achieve happiness."

DEATH ENIGMA

"Death is the only phenomenon of the universe which we have not been able to unravel; not even scientists cannot fully grasp what this experience means." Most aspects of life have been explored, analyzed, and discovered, but death intrigues humanity without explaining the true meaning. Men have contaminated everything else on this planet, but death remains a pure and stable aspect of life. *"Death is inexplicable, the only enigma for all humanity because nobody has ever come back from the dead to give details about this natural phenomenon."* We attempt to describe it in shades of meaning, but it is virtually impossible to comprehend. Studies in Psychology have explained to us that birth is the first step on the way to the ultimate ending of death. We don't know about death, but it seems to be an exciting profile for those who believe that death is not the final stage but rather the opening to a new and better life. Some people think we need to behave ourselves well, being a good human in exchange for an everlasting life after death. We all know that we will die. Still we don't know when or how this event will occur. Therefore, be emotionally prepared for spiritual concerns at the moment to face death. You recognize your mistakes, think about other people suffering, so death does not surprise you full of hatred and resentment. Let's live in peace

and harmony, forgive people who have offended you, and accept those things you cannot change while you are alive.

"Death could be a door to a new life."

"We know one day we all will die, but we don't know when or how this event will occur."

GENEROSITY

"Generous people are the ones who give the most without expecting gratitude." As human beings, we must fulfill "a divine mission of helping others". Positive action leads a life filled with happiness and harmony to the generous and their beliefs. Generosity is a feeling of giving help without expecting anything in return, keeping open hearts to people in need, to develop a happy sensation of endless possibilities. Be generous out of convenience. Humanity need solidarity, and their suffering concern you, then "donate what you have, not what you have leftover, it is the real act of generosity." In contrast to a selfish person, a generous person helps others instinctively while opening their hearts because they are conscious of their needs. A helpful person transforms their life into a symbol of love through love for humanity.

"Always donate as a symbol of love, so what you give will not be material but love."

"Generosity is a virtue filled with great satisfaction. The capacity by doing good deeds will help you feel supportive and happy throughout your whole life."

REJOICE IN FAMILY

"Rejoicing with members of your family is part of daily life."
Making mistakes and resolving misunderstandings are common in all families. Still, the most important thing is to be united by love, care, and respect for each other in their ideals to forgive such mistakes. We know your family is the most critical and influential environment that a person needs for safety and support in this life. Having a family is a treasure to care for and hold in the face of adversity and rejoicing moments. The family deserves your total effort to achieve love, not just in words but in actions. *"Forgiveness and communication are powerful tools for reestablishing grateful family relationships."* *"Don't build up resentment; it creates bad vibrations and damages your environment."* Permanent resentment creates negative vibes which are impossible to escape. Our responsibility as parents is to teach our children proper values and love them with joy. The old proverb *"blood is thicker than water"* teaches us that siblings will remain connected throughout their lifetime. *"It is important to recognize that no family problem is so big as to resolve the inconvenience through love."*

RENOUNCE TO THE SIN

One of my favorite writers, Jorge Luis Borges, said: *"I have committed the worst sins that a man can commit. I have not been happy."* He did not make happiness his priority. I agree with this phrase because when you don't believe in yourself, you won't have the necessary awareness to keep you away from committing great sins. Abandon yourself means inflicting damage and hurting your inner spirit. This unawareness/negligence is human nature. *"You must not sin of being unhappy, instead perceive the positive divine messages from the Universe."* Create your own story according to your values by being authentic. You are a human with virtues and defects but true to yourself to walk on the right path of happiness. Your path is the road to follow through guided by the heart will lead you to the goal of divine truth more quickly than the mind could because the mind is constantly changing, listening to your heart will reach your objective of happiness much more rapidly. Unfortunately, your mind is often in a state of confusion. Still, your gut contains your divine spirit and is overflowing with spiritual goodness. The reallocation of the soul is inside your heart, but the soul's consciousness is throughout your whole body.

KARMA

"Karma is like your breath; do a person's actions generate the force to perpetuate transmigration and in its ethical consequences to determine the nature of the person's next existence." connects you to the spiritual world; it exists in all humans, whether good or bad, in all people who are filled with good thoughts and positive feelings; karma can be pure and clean. Good karma lives in people who have light in their souls. *"The mind can transform your Karma from negative to positive, only if your Karma is purified."* Your karma will reach harmony with the spiritual level if you can purify your Karma through good deeds and positive thoughts. It is essential not to try to involve yourself in other people's Karma. Such involvement will make your life heavy and difficult. If you make other people's problems your issues, you will suffer greatly, and you will create an emotional imbalance that will take away your peace. Meditation can help you purify your karma in many ways.

CHAKRAS

They are centers of energy located in the human body; there are seven primary chakras and two secondary ones related to the acupuncture points. *"Chakras can help manage your potential for projecting and receiving positive energy."* If you maintain a suitable energetic level in your body, the development of your daily activities will become more positive, similar to performing that physical exercise. After doing exercise, you feel more energetic. Chakras work as the energy you have in your inner self by connecting your chakras with your dreams to achieve natural and relaxed energy flow.

DIVINE LOVE

Divine love is based on freedom of mind, respecting both their values and ideals. True love does not mean that you need to sacrifice anything; it is living and breathing with liberty as a *"divine love."* Divine love never binds you to another person; instead, it liberates you and expands your possibilities for happiness. When you feel the freedom, you think of the divine obligation to do something positive for your inner peace. Real love does not manipulate or force you to feel happy; it flows freely and occurs when both enjoy spending time together without obligation. Love is marvelous when it flows freely and naturally from the heart. *Divine love* doesn't bind you, and love opens up the world of infinite truth by liberating you from all mistaken and irrational concepts of love in general.

"Love is the only feeling that is true and real. If you want to know what real love is, you need to discover your inner."

SPIRITUALITY AND SCIENCE

When we compare Spirituality to Science, we can see no existing connection or attraction between them.

1. *God is the fundamental basis of the spiritual world, but Science doesn't need a God to offer humanity all the practical tools for unraveling the mysteries of the exterior world;*
2. *Spiritually connect humans to the feelings of life and the significance of existence on earth, but Science depends on external experiments;*
3. *Spirituality is on an internal search and exploration, but a scientist often discovers powers that can threaten the world; and*
4. *A spiritual explorer discovers the powers that mold their own life to a melancholy life filled with divine reality. Still scientists search the external world to experiment.*

The relationship between science and spirituality should have mutual acceptance and proper understanding. It would be foolish on your part to hope for the same truths or knowledge offered by science in spirituality. It should establish the same goals when analyzing either one.

"A person who is attached to material things will always remain a prisoner of ambition. The end product to ambition is always wealth filled with pain, sadness, and loneliness."

THE SPIRITUAL HEART

"It is better to meditate in the heart instead of the mind." The mind offers distraction, while the heart is your peaceful world, so if you meditate with your soul, you will acquire the capacity for identifying with the divine light of happiness which remains. The heart center is pure, tender, full of love and peace and is the divinity. At first you identify with god and truth and then convert it into your reality by under this identification.

"There is no greater truth than a pure heart. It opens a world in which you surrender yourself to the divine world full of love."

"We don't deceive our heart with traps; it is the heart which traps the reason with significant feelings." "The soul only surrenders itself to love and it is our proper identity."

PURIFY YOUR MIND

The mind is fragile, imprecise, impure, and often a victim of doubt or fear. *"All negative thoughts attack the mind as a first reaction, and sometimes the mind rejects these negative impulses by nature that it is attracted to negativity."* To purify your mind, you must trust your inner thoughts from your heart. Your inner thoughts are not imaginary; they are coherent and logically follow that you must always trust your heart's messages. The heart, unlike the mind, does not open itself to impure ideas. The soul is the correct answer and offers the surest way to happiness and divinity. The heart is much purer than the mind because it feels and embraces the divine world. Spiritual life is accurate because it has real feelings. The mind creates illusions that you want to achieve by obtaining material things. Delusion is not deep or divine, because fantasy is fleeting, and the only real thing in life is eternal love.

"Tranquility brings to your mind a new world filled with divine light that will grow and lead you to happiness." Prepare your mind for only a moment; it will feel like something divine is developing in your natural purity. Do not think about obtaining immediate results, and focus your mind on your hope to reach and achieve great results. *"If you encourage all your positive energy into your spiritual meditation, your life will be illuminated by the magnetic power of possibility."* When you meditate, you don't think about the absolute object meditation to free yourself from all thoughts. Only if there is no thought you can reach the highest level of reality, that highest level of meditation brings you to the light.

WISDOM

The great sages of history are highly intellectual people, well-educated and brilliant, with broad knowledge in all aspects of life. *"Wisdom supposedly has the answers to all our questions, and they coherently develop their mind with the uncommon ability to balance emotions and feelings." "Being wise is a virtue worth its weight in pure gold."* We are not born wise, but we can understand deep questions of life by discovering ourselves, investigating in our own life where those inner secrets are that help to find our place in life. Wisdom will help you to lead a fulfilling life to be able to distinguish between real and unreal. *"If you are at peace with yourself, you are a sage because you have discovered a way of making yourself happy." "This is real wisdom."* Even simple things in life require wisdom, but it is prevalent to live under stress trying to solve every problem you face in a haphazardly random manner. *"Wisdom advises you to think before you act. You must remain calm and meditate before deciding to improve your health for creating a more rewarding life for yourself."* Being wise about your life and destiny will lead you not to care about those things which cause you an emotional imbalance. You can learn day by day that everything flows naturally, knows how to grow emotionally, and accept items that are impossible to change.

PURE AND DIVINE SOUL

In the deepest part of the soul are elements not touched by the exterior world. *"Meditation is the best way for reaching the goodness contained within the heart and soul, but only spiritual people can perceive and feel the soul attain true happiness."* The purity of your heart and soul will lead you to life's greatest secret where there is absolute divinity, which is the guiding light that will bring you to happiness. Exploring yourself, you will discover these divine and pure virtues to recognize your soul in all its most profound wonders. If you try to accomplish this, you will love yourself much more and get the wisdom necessary for choosing the correct path to happiness in your life. Spiritual life creates your spiritual world so simple: "individual -soul-heart" - to follow the messages in your heart by discovering what is natural and divine in the road to happiness. Spiritual life makes you believe in yourself and will give you the power and wisdom to accept those things you cannot change to embrace your talents. Exploring your spiritual life world means having confidence in yourself and elevating your self-esteem, knowing who you are, strong, positive, and ready to face life's challenges with calmness and wisdom.

"Trust in the beating of your heart; each heartbeat is a message of love, every message of love brings hope, and a hopeful feeling can light the road to your truth and real life."

THE SPIRITUAL LEVEL

There are levels of spirituality to reach a spiritual level followed on a step-by-step basis in emotional balance. You begin knowing yourself, and by trying to enter your soul, you let your heart speak to you instead of relying solely on your mind. Finally you learn how to detach yourself from the material world. You know to reach a high level of reflection in meditation by achieving an emotional balance and accept life as it comes. You don't suffer or feel desperate, and nobody can offend you or touch you with negative thoughts. Negative ideas change to positive energy, and you attain a realm in which only peace and divinity exist. To reach this level of spirituality requires acquiring a lot of self-knowledge and wisdom plus meditation exercises and mantras. Spirituality is a real encounter with the divine secrets of light, peace, and harmony. It is impossible to change the world, but you can change yourself by focussing on what is real, and those things that can change. As a human bound to make mistakes in life, you will realize that nature flows on its course, and you will not feel disillusioned or desperate when you fail. Remember, take control of your life, hold the reins of your soul and heart to keep in an emotional balance. In a couple, the spiritual level is the key for any relationship; respecting each other will attain the highest level of peace and divinity. Accepting each other as they are will be the way to reach the spiritual level.

"Spirituality is a real encounter with the divine secrets of light, peace, and harmony."

"The heart feels love inside and transforms it into long-lasting positive experiences."

"The heart is strengthened through personal life experiences which contribute to emotional growth and increased wisdom."

LIVE IN PEACE

"Peace is the tranquility of a human being to live full of love and in an emotional balance." Live in peace, letting your heart and soul look in your inner self, feel calm and meditate quickly find it. Peace does not get along with noise, violence, or negative people; you will feel peace when you let go of the difficult situations you cannot resolve. *"Peace only exists in the feeling of love and calmness in the soul. To relax and find harmony in your inner peace, you should practice yoga."* The worldwide balance is far from successful because of wars, natural disasters, pandemics, social, political, and economic issues. The world is suffering the consequences of human materialism. The lack of knowledge regarding what is destroying the planet's environment, and the worst is "the human carelessness of those who have the power to find solutions positively and precisely," but they ignore the consequences. We all are humans created by God for achieving love and peace, regardless of race, religion, or social condition. Let's make our planet a better place to live.

LOVE IS DIVINE

"The heart is strengthened through personal life experiences, which contribute to emotional growth and increased wisdom." A strong heart has the power to place life's difficulties on the side and let things go for the sake of their happiness. The heart feels love inside and transforms it into long-lasting positive experiences. Nothing and nobody can erase those moments of joy that the nucleus has experienced. You will keep these pleasant memories and will stay in your heart forever. Love in its authentic divinity furnishes your soul with peace to attain through concerted meditation, which requires some time and patience for most of you to accept genuine love. Heartbeats are divine messages that can transmit sensations of joy or anguish. Sometimes you understand the religious messages. You always know a heart is never wrong; therefore, you must let yourself guide by this beat. Later you will confirm to follow the heart's path. Heartbeat is your alarm which wakes you up in life and tells you not to become distracted by things happening in your material environment.

"Divine love is the total acceptance spirit to feel it; everything in your life will flow easily to balance your life."

"Dreams are divine messages which are consequences of our subconscious thoughts and emotions."

"Trust in your heart, and you will find the hidden truth, but which will reveal itself with total freedom."

Connie C. Torres

LET THINGS FLOW

You must avoid thinking that all things in life should happen the way you expect; instead you should focus your energy on positive things and flow naturally. The key to wisdom is to understand that life flows. The only attitude that will help you always be at peace is to let life flow by nature. For everything to flow as it must, you cannot place obstacles in your way or worry about those things which you cannot change because these will happen. People who let life flow naturally have learned to harness cosmic energy and possess the divine willingness to erase life's moments of sorrow. Don't stay stuck on past errors but concentrate on making positive changes in the present, leading you to a happier future. One of the most challenging things to accept in life's situations that happen affect you and make you emotionally grow. You learn from human mistakes- the power of acceptance to life's flow connecting to those positive aspects you place in your heart. Your heartbeats will tell you the truth, and your reality can make your world more positive to trust in what your heart tells you. Real love occurs when you accept life as it comes-both excellent and bad events.

FOUNDATION FOR YOUR SPIRITUAL GROWTH

Your spiritual growth will begin when:

1. *You understand that you control your feelings;*
2. *You are the one who knows what you need;*
3. *You are capable of maintaining an emotional balance in any situation;*
4. *Your spiritual world starts to blossom;*
5. *You learn that material things merely have a secondary role in life;*
6. *You nurture your affections because these are the most vibrant feelings that exist;*
7. *You are concerned with the well-being of others;*
8. *You dare not to place values on material things and open your mind to the spiritual world; and*
9. *You reach a higher level of reality where nothing can reach you, nor touch you, nor hurt you, nor cause you injury.*

REFLECTION

Reflection is a meditation on your thoughts, making an analysis of your emotions and sharpening your feelings. You meditate about situations that have caused you to feel dissatisfied and reflect by focusing your positive energy on solving the crisis. Reflection is part of the spiritual growth that will lead you to new facets of life that will enrich your experience positively and precisely. Life offers you the opportunities to reflect daily, to calm down for a moment, and establish the proper direction for your ideas, which become scrambled in your mind. You should not live an empty life filled with unreal things which that will cause you unhappiness. Take control of your thoughts, especially when you are not on a balanced path in life. Reflection will help you remain peacefully, living in your inner self to light up your days full of happiness.

"Reflection is the key to feel in harmony through meditation. Meditation offers not only a way to meet spiritual truth but also means to achieve an emotional balance, physical wellbeing, as well as spiritual development in all aspects of life."

REFLECTION ON LIFE

Love instead of hate.
Peace instead of war.
Serenity instead of disturbance.
Forgive instead of punishing.
Friend instead of an enemy.
Voice instead of silence.
Good instead of evil.
Generous instead of selfish.
Happy instead of sad.
Brave instead of a coward.
Confidence instead of fear.
True instead of lies.
Sincere instead of false.
Calm instead of anxious.

"Reflection opens the doors to a world full of love."

"Love grows in our inner self, giving unconditional love in abundance will come back to you when you least expect it, and it will stay with you forever."

"Real love will provide you with more than you thought you were capable of giving. The more you love, the more benefits you will give yourself".

"Only you decide your happiness. If you search for calm, you will find it is the leader of your thoughts through reflection."

Connie C. Torres

THE PANDEMIC 2020

The pandemic has focused the world's attention on microbial influences on human life. COVID-19, first identified in Wuhan, China 2019, has caused unbalance in social, economic, and political issues. Humanity has experienced many epidemics through the years, this is not new, but for people experiencing it for the first time is an incredible catastrophe. The Population has been affected in all aspects, creating universal chaos, very difficult to control and stop the spread of the virus, loss of lives, and permanent jobs. Today a society lives in a pause, suffering, then tries again to get up and wishes to say goodbye to this calamity. As humans we must be united and contribute to all the protocols to stop the spread of this virus, being aware we are all humans. We owe each other solidarity to emerge victorious from this world crisis, in which we all are involved. The time to raise awareness came with the pandemic; if we learn, we will be better human beings.

I DECIDED TO BE FREE

"I decided to be free" from my inner soul, searching for happiness to let you know life can be better for all of you. The freedom of mind will become you as a human being living a real-life with no fears, as a unique person who needs the courage to face the external world as it comes. "I decided to be free to find my inner sense of living, my soul, my heart, to live as real as I am. "Freedom is having a high level of self-confidence, making your dreams come true, embracing your feelings and your thoughts." "I decided to free myself of mental prisons." Sometimes "freedom" is misunderstood by the false sense of irresponsibility and care about your actions; instead, "freedom" is based on your feelings as a unique human at a high level of self-confidence.

"Decide to be free of mind, be yourself, and be authentic. You could start doing things you love to do to make you feel happy inside, things you've never done before, so you will finally feel relaxed and your world itself will change."

Feel the freedom of your feelings, think and decide. Confidence is the only way you can fly via your dreams and feel happy with every step you take in the direction of happiness."

"Deciding to be free is growing as a human being and feeling happy. It is about raising your self-esteem by feeling in harmony, making decisions that benefit your own life in this material world."

"Smile as soon as you wake up in the morning, It will be the first step towards deciding to be happy as a human being."

"Life does not have to be what is in your dreams; just live it as it comes."

Connie C. Torres

TO THE READERS

Writing makes me feel free and comfortable; it is like feeling related to others through writing. It is very grateful for me to encourage you to find your freedom by embracing your happiness. My own experience was full of sadness and tears, but I finally decided to be myself, confident without any expectations. I chose not to feel hurt by others' behaviors, just let life flow to live my positive daily life, which helps me to find an emotional balance according to my heart's feelings. I don't worry anymore about any situation I can't resolve. Still I focus on the ones I can solve by spreading my energy in a positive manner to reflect on others to balance my environment. I mean it wholeheartedly when I say this book is for you because my concern is your happiness, sharing my feelings for those who need it. I dream that everyone finds happiness. Thanks to the readers!! Those who decided to be happy and motivated by the first edition, there are no words to express how I feel inside of my heart. *"Your happiness is my happiness, and my decision is only my positive attitude that I assume in each situation, letting love flow in my daily life and thankfulness for being alive.*

"Don't go behind anybody or anything, relax, just smile and be calm because dreams will come to you as real as you desire having a positive attitude." Connie C. Torres

I decided to be free

Decidí ser Feliz

J'ai décidé d'être heureux

DEDICATION

I dedicate this book to all readers searching for finding their inner-self, exploring their souls to achieve a spiritual growth- my joyful meaning of life for those who have the chance to read it. I decided to be free, encouraging you to become a better human, keeping the balance between the spiritual and material world. My essence in this book is for people who embrace life as it comes, to follow their dreams on their path of happiness. I am delighted to share a part of myself with you. Thanks family and friends who love and support me. Deciding to be free is awful. Thank you to my daughter Connie D. Torres and her best friend Becky McNickle for their help, and being part of the team "I decided to be free."

PHOTO GALLERIES

I Decided to Be Free Around The World

EUROPE - FRANCE

The Louvre Museum, Paris

The Eiffel Tower, Paris

The Concorde Square, Paris

The Arch of Triumph, Paris

UNITED KINGDOM - ENGLAND

The Buckingham Palace, London

The London Eye, London

The London Bridge, England

UNITED STATES - NEW YORK

Times Square, Manhattan

New York City View, Brooklyn

The Statue of Liberty, New York

ILLINOIS

The Millennium Park, Chicago

NEVADA

The City Center, Las Vegas

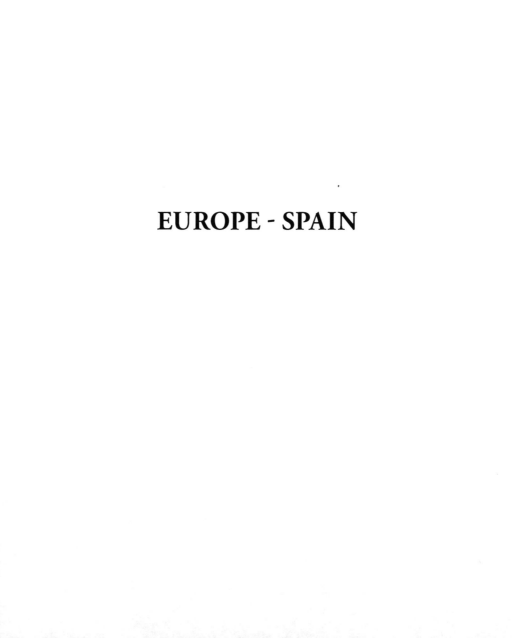

EUROPE - SPAIN

The Sacred Family, Barcelona

Barceloneta, Barcelona

The Real Palace, Madrid

The Door of Alcalá, Madrid

San Sebastián de los Reyes, Spain

EUROPE - ITALY

The Coliseum, Rome

The Vatican City, Italy

The Grand Canal, Venice

The Rialto Bridge, Venice

Ancona Port, Italy

Romeo and Juliet City, Verona, Italy

EUROPE - NETHERLANDS

The Rembrandt Monument, Amsterdam

The Rokin Canal, Amsterdam

Madurodam, a miniature replica of Amsterdam City.

Dubrovnik, Croatia

Santorini, Greece

Mykonos, Greece

SOUTH AMERICA - COLOMBIA

Cali, Colombia

La Piedra del Penol, Guatape

The Botero Plaza, Medellín

Panoramic View of Cali, Colombia

Armenia, Quindio

URUGUAY

The Port of Montevideo

ARGENTINA

The Obelisco, Buenos Aires

The Monument to the Flag, Rosario, Argentina

CARIBBEAN ISLANDS - BAHAMAS

The Atlantis Resorts, Nassau

MEXICO

Cancun Beach, Quintana Rod

ECUADOR

Guayaquil Panoramic View

The Pandemic 2020, New York

The Six Times of Happiness

SOCIAL MEDIA

https://www.facebook.com/cctorresdecidiserfeliz

https://www.facebook.com/Idecidedtobefree/

https://www.facebook.com/libro.henrynelsonelultimoromantico/

https://www.facebook.com/Y-donde-est%C3%A1-el-chiste--22114
7728242725

https://www.facebook.com/Decidí-SER-FELIZ-Cd-Music-14660
97593468957/

https://www.facebook.com/VAMOS-MUNDO-CD-Connie-
Torres-109900387111302/

https://www.facebook.com/connie.c.torres

https://www.facebook.com/connie.torres.39948

https://www.facebook.com/cctorresdecidiserfeliz

https://www.facebook.com/search/top/?q=The%20Six%20Times%20
f%20Happiness%20Shopping

conniectorres@gmail.com

Printed in the United States
by Baker & Taylor Publisher Services